001.9
SIM

Simon, Seymour.

Strange mysteries
from around the
world.

$16.00

450318

| DATE | | | |
|---|---|---|---|
| | | | |
| | | | |
| | | | |
| | | | |
| | | | |
| | | | |
| | | | |
| | | | |
| | | | |
| | | | |
| | | | |
| | | | |

# STRANGE MYSTERIES

FROM AROUND THE WORLD

## SEYMOUR SIMON

MORROW JUNIOR BOOKS
NEW YORK

With my love to Michael and Debra, and
their daughter and my granddaughter, Chloe

Photo Credits

Permission to use the following photographs and art is gratefully acknowledged: pages 3, 29, Bettmann Archive; pages 8, 10, 14, UPI/Bettmann; pages 20, 24, 25, Public Archives of Nova Scotia; page 34 and jacket, National Museum of the American Indian; page 45, Alfred Pasieka/Science Source; page 48, Greg Schaler/Science Source; page 51, National Optical Astronomy Observatories; page 57, U.S. Geological Survey Photographic Library.

Printed in the United States of America.

1  2  3  4  5  6  7  8  9  10

Library of Congress Cataloging-in-Publication Data
Simon, Seymour.
Strange mysteries from around the world / Seymour Simon.
p.  cm.
Summary: Describes nine strange natural phenomena and possible explanations for them, including the day it rained frogs, an atomic explosion that occurred forty years before the atom bomb, and an eerie crystal skull.
ISBN 0-688-14636-8
1. Curiosities and wonders—Juvenile literature.  [1. Curiosities and wonders.]  I. Title.
AG243.S57 1997   001.9′4—dc20   96-2693   CIP  AC

# CONTENTS

# INTRODUCTION

Everybody enjoys a mystery. The stranger the mystery, the more we enjoy it. And our enjoyment is even greater when we know that the mystery really happened!

This book is about strange mysteries that are true: days that frogs and fish rained down from the skies; a buried treasure whose location is known but that has never been recovered; the strange disappearance of an entire ship's crew; what seems to be an atomic explosion that occurred forty years before the invention of the atom bomb; and others. We know that these things happened, but we still don't know the reason why.

But there are many strange things that occur in the world around us. Some of the mysteries in this book are so strange as to baffle the imagination. Some of them may never be solved.

# CHAPTER ONE

# IT'S RAINING
# FROGS AND FISH

When it's raining heavily, some people say that it's "pouring cats and dogs." Of course, that's only an expression. Cats and dogs really don't rain down from the sky. (Although there may be *poodles* in the street.) But don't be too sure that it never rains animals.

Here is a quote from the July 12, 1873, issue of the magazine *Scientific American:* "A shower of frogs, which darkened the air and covered the ground for a long distance, is the reported result of a recent rainstorm at Kansas City, Mo."

And this is by no means the only reported observation of animal showers. Here is a report from an 1841 issue of an English magazine called *The Athenaeum:* "During a heavy thunderstorm, the rain poured down in torrents mixed with half-melted ice, and, incredible as it may appear, hundreds of small fishes and frogs in great abundance descended with the torrents of rain. The fish were from half an inch to two inches long.... Many were picked up alive. The frogs jumped away as fast as they could, but the bulk of them were killed by the fall on the hard pavement."

The idea of living things raining down from the sky is difficult to believe. But from ancient times up to the present there have been reports of showers of one kind or another of animals or plants.

In olden times, these living showers were thought to be supernatural. People believed in magic and witches. They believed in good and evil omens. People must have been frightened or pleased, depending upon what rained down. But whatever animal or plant rained down, it certainly seemed to be a miracle.

There are still many stories of strange animal showers. The reports are often printed in magazines or newspapers of the time. Let's look at some of these reports and then see if they can be explained in any scientific way.

Here is a report from *Scientific American,* February 21, 1891: "In some parts of Randolph County, Virginia, this winter, the crust of the snow has been covered two or three times with worms.... A square foot of snow can scarcely be found some days without a dozen of these worms on it."

Another report from *Scientific American,* in 1877, tells about a rain of snakes in Memphis, Tennessee. "Thousands of little reptiles, ranging from a foot to eighteen inches in length, were distributed all over the southern part of the city."

A plague of frogs startled the diners in this print. In olden times, people believed that the frogs came from supernatural causes.

A shower of frogs was reported in a 1939 issue of the English journal *Meteorological Magazine*. "Mr. E. Ettles, superintendent of the municipal swimming pool, stated that about 4:30 P.M. he was caught in a heavy shower of rain and, while hurrying to shelter, heard behind him a sound as of the falling of lumps of mud. Turning, he was amazed to see hundreds of tiny frogs falling on the concrete path around the bath. Later, many more were found to have fallen on the grass nearby."

Even turtles seem to have fallen from the sky. Here is a report from a 1930 issue of *Nature* magazine: "During a severe hailstorm in Vicksburg (U.S.A.)...a gopher turtle, 6 inches by 8 inches, and entirely encased in ice, fell with the hail."

In 1949, a long article appeared in the magazine *Science*. The author, A. D. Bajkov, was a biologist working for the Department of Wild Life and Fisheries. Here is part of his eyewitness report of what happened in Marksville, Louisiana:

"In the morning of October 23, 1947, between seven and eight o'clock, fish ranging from two to nine inches in length fell on the streets and in the yards.... I was in the restaurant with my wife having breakfast, when the waitress informed us that fish were falling from the sky. We went immediately to collect some of the fish.

"The director of the bank said that he had discovered that fish had fallen by hundreds in his yard, and in the adjacent yard. The cashier of the bank and two merchants were struck by falling fish as they walked toward their places of business about 7:45 A.M. There were spots on Main Street averaging one fish per square yard. Automobiles and trucks were running over them. Fish also fell on the roofs of houses."

Bajkov goes on to identify the fish as bass, sunfish, minnows, and shad. These were all freshwater fish found in local waters. The fish that fell that day in Louisiana were absolutely fresh and fit to be eaten, although Bajkov doesn't say whether he ate any of the fish or how they tasted.

As recently as February 1994, thousands of small fish were found in the Australian desert, flapping about in parking lots and on roads. The fish were found just after a rainstorm. A few days later, thousands more fish, this time slightly larger, were found in puddles after five inches of overnight rain. From 1988 to 1994, there have been three fish falls in this area.

Looking at these reports, it seems clear that at least some actually happened. If these reports are true, then what possible explanations could they have?

In the stories of worms, caterpillars, or insects found on snow or the surface of the ground, heavy rains or melting snows are often mentioned. Perhaps the soil became waterlogged and the worms or insects were driven to the surface from their underground homes.

In most of the other animal showers, windstorms or tornadoes probably lifted the animals into the air and then dropped them some distance away. For example, tornadoes are known to have lifted houses, cars, and even a train locomotive. It is not surprising that a tornado would also have the force to lift fish, frogs, or even a turtle.

However, there are still some strange things that cannot be explained. First, many of the animal showers report only one kind of animal falling. Why should a whirlwind select only frogs one day and not a combination of animals: fish, frogs, turtles? Second, all the animals that fall are often about the same size. Shouldn't a whirlwind pick up animals of different sizes? Third, the animals often fall without any plants or sand along with them. Shouldn't a whirlwind pick up some of the material surrounding an animal?

While we may not know all the answers to the mysteries of falling animals, this much is sure. The next time someone says that it is raining frogs and fish, you better go out and have a look. He or she may be right.

## CHAPTER TWO

# BIG BANG IN SIBERIA

At 7:17 in the morning of June 30, 1908, the biggest explosion ever recorded anywhere on the earth took place close to the Tunguska River, in a distant part of Siberia. The big bang blew down trees for dozens of miles in all directions. People and animals were knocked off their feet four hundred miles from the center of the blast. The shocks from the explosion were recorded all around the earth. The explosion was so bright that it made the sun appear dark by contrast. The London *Times* of July 4, 1908, reported on "the remarkable ruddy glows which have been seen on many nights lately,…seen as far as Berlin."

The Siberian big bang of 1908 occurred many years before the United States set off the first atomic bomb. Yet some scientists say that the blast could only have been caused by some sort of atomic explosion. Other explanations range from spaceships from other worlds to a comet or meteorite crash to a meeting with what astronomers call a black hole.

The place in Siberia is so far away from any roads that it wasn't until 1927, nineteen years after the blast, that a Soviet scientist, L. A. Kulick, visited the spot. He found trees splintered and burned in an area twenty miles across. He also discovered ten small craters near the blast center, none more than fifty yards across.

Eyewitness accounts later were collected by another Soviet scientist, E. L. Krinov. He reported that many witnesses hundreds of miles away saw an object fall across the sky a few seconds before the blast.

A peasant who lived about forty miles from the center of the explosion had these recollections. He first saw a large sheet of flame that lasted just an instant. Then the sky grew dark and the blast threw him off an open porch.

The nights following the explosion were unusually bright in Siberia, the rest of Russia, and in Europe as well. Even at midnight it was possible to read a newspaper.

Recently, some scientists have pointed out many features of the Siberian blast that resemble those of an atom- or hydrogen-bomb explosion. For example, an excess of radioactivity was found in the area. Also, the trees at the center of the explosion were stripped of bark and branches. They looked like telephone poles, just like the trees seen after the atomic-bomb blast at Hiroshima.

In 1959, British Atomic Energy scientists raised the possibility that the Siberian blast was an atomic explosion due to natural causes. They said that a meteorite or comet plunging into the earth may have contained enough of the material needed to produce an atomic blast. The heat of the meteor's entry into earth's atmosphere might have set off the explosion. But this is only a theory; there is no evidence that this actually happened.

In 1961, a Soviet science writer wrote an article in which he claimed that the explosion was caused by an atomic or hydrogen bomb carried to earth aboard a spaceship from another planet.

An even more fantastic explanation came from two other Soviet science writers in a 1964 article. They proposed that the explosion was from a laser beam launched from the star 61 Cygni. It seemed that the good folks on 61 Cygni had slightly mis-calculated the power of the laser beam. Instead of a friendly hello

from space, the arrival of the laser beam resulted in a world-shaking explosion. Needless to say, few people have accepted this fanciful explanation.

In 1965, a Nobel Prize–winning scientist, Dr. Willard Libby, suggested that the blast was due to the fall of a meteor made of antimatter. Antimatter is a substance that is just like regular matter, except that each of its particles has an opposite electrical charge. If a piece of antimatter touched a piece of matter, there would be a violent explosion.

In 1967, an important Soviet scientific journal printed an article by a member of the Soviet Academy of Sciences who had been on an expedition to the blast site in Siberia. He said that the growth

rings of trees that lived through the blast definitely showed a nearby source of radioactivity. He concluded that the effects were those of a nuclear explosion such as that of a hydrogen bomb.

Still another theory was proposed in 1973, by two scientists at the University of Texas. They said that the explosion was caused by a black hole. The matter in a black hole is squeezed together so tightly that even a tiny black hole is incredibly heavy—a few million tons. If such a black hole were to hit our planet, it would go right through. According to this theory, the black hole exited from somewhere in the mid–Atlantic Ocean.

The nuclear-explosion idea was proposed again by an Israeli scientist, Professor Ari Ben-Menahem, in 1975. He looked at shock records from around the world at the time. Even though the explosion seemed to have gone off high in the air, blast waves traveled around the world both in the air and within the earth. He concluded that the explosion took place five miles above the ground and was probably a nuclear missile from space with a force of ten to fifteen million tons of TNT.

Most scientists don't go along with all the ideas of a nuclear blast, a laser beam, visitors from other planets, antimatter, or black holes. They prefer to think that the explosion was caused by the fall of a comet. This theory was originally put forth in the early 1930s by Fred Whipple, an American astronomer.

A comet is made up of a head and a tail. The head is made up of dust, rocks, and ice—like a dirty snowball. The tail is made up of dust and gases. According to Whipple, the comet slowed down when it entered the earth's atmosphere. This made it gain energy, and it exploded in the air. The bright nights after the explosion were caused by the dust in the comet's tail that was left in the atmosphere. This theory, however, does not account for the radioactivity in the area.

A Czechoslovakian scientist, L. Kresak, supported the idea that the explosion in Siberia was caused by a comet. But his theory was that a huge boulder split away from the comet Encke. The boulder entered the atmosphere and became so hot that it exploded.

Was the big bang in Siberia the result of a comet or a meteor hitting the earth, as most scientists now believe? Was it an atomic explosion that occurred in nature? Was it the result of a black hole? Or was the blast really caused by some unknown visitors from Mars or beyond? It's unlikely that this mystery will ever be solved to everyone's satisfaction.

CHAPTER THREE

# WALKING ON FIRE

Can you imagine people walking barefoot on red-hot coals without burning their feet?

Fire walking is not a fake. It has been observed time and time again by many people, including scientists. And nobody is exactly sure why the fire walkers are not seriously injured.

Fire walking is a ceremony practiced in different parts of the world, including India, Japan, North Africa, and some islands in the South Pacific. The walking itself takes many forms. Most often the fire walkers move swiftly over a layer of hot coals spread at the bottom of a shallow trench. In other places, the walkers stride across red-hot stones or through an open fire. The coals or rocks are so hot that they can burn through a thick pair of boots with no difficulty.

An Australian reporter, John Godwin, describes in his book *This Baffling World* one exciting incident of fire walking that he

This fire walker is moving through a bed of glowing coals, as part of a ceremony in Pakistan. The coals are kept hot by attendants who fan the embers.

witnessed in 1959. It took place in Bora Bora, an island in the South Pacific. Like a circus coming to town, the fire walking was announced several days in advance. When the day came, several hundred people had gathered together to view the entertainment.

The fire pit was about forty feet long and twenty feet wide. In the pit, large rocks were lying on a bed of burning logs. The fire had been burning for the past two days. The rocks were red-hot and gave off heat waves that made the air shimmer.

Several people tried to stand at the edge of the fire pit, but the heat was too great and they had to step back. A native dropped a few rags onto the rocks in the pit. In a few seconds, the rags burst into flame and became ashes.

Finally, the fire walkers appeared. There were eight of them, all from Tahiti, a nearby island. They allowed their feet to be examined by anyone who asked. There were no coatings of any kind on the soles of their feet.

Drums started to beat, and it was time for the fire walking. The eight men picked up palm branches and began to sing. They formed a single line and marched toward the pit.

At the edge of the pit, the first man in line stopped for a moment and gazed down at the red-hot rocks. After an instant, he walked into the trench, stepping from rock to rock. Halfway through the length of the pit, he raised his palm branch. One by one, the other men followed him into the pit. They walked quickly but did not run.

At the far end of the pit, the men came out and rested for a few minutes. Then they started to make the return trip, again in single file. They walked without hesitating or stumbling and without making any sounds.

As soon as the performance was over, the fire walkers were surrounded by onlookers. Their bodies were drenched in sweat. They held up their feet to be examined. The soles were black with charcoal, but underneath the charcoal the skin was unburned. Some of the fire walkers had a few blisters on their ankles, but that was all. There were no burns or other signs of what they had just been through.

Arthur C. Clarke, the well-known science author, photographed a fire-walking ceremony in Ceylon. He describes how a pile of glowing embers was pushed into a mass about twelve feet long and two inches deep. Several hundred people participated in the fire walking. They walked or danced across the fire bed. Some sank into the embers up to their ankles. None showed any signs of pain.

Acts of fire walking also have taken place in the United States and England, as well as in the Far East. For example, a number of years ago Robert Ripley, of "Believe-It-or-Not" fame, promoted a fire-walking exhibition in Rockefeller Center in New York. An Indian man named Kuda Box attempted to walk the length of a twenty-foot trench of hot coals. He had to leap out after walking only ten feet, but even that length should have burned his feet badly. Yet his feet showed no burns or blisters.

An article about fire walking in the January 1974 issue of the magazine *Natural History* describes how fire walking is a religious ceremony in some small villages in India. The walkers are ordinary people who choose to walk the fire to prove their faith and purity to the goddess Kali. They hope that Kali will cure their own illnesses or those of a close relative. Parents of a sick child will often carry the child through the fire.

The only preparations the fire walkers make are spiritual ones. They live by themselves in the village temple for several days before the fire-walking ceremony. They do not talk to anyone except other fire walkers.

The fire pit is twenty yards long and filled with hot coals. The walkers have to travel the entire pit seven times during the ceremony. They believe that only those who lack faith will be injured.

The *Natural History* article notes that the fire-walking ceremony had been performed many times before in the village. But this time the walking ended in failure and injury. Ten of the fifteen walkers were badly burned. The villagers were confused and upset. They believed that they were no longer under the protection of their gods.

Despite the occasional failures and injuries during some fire-walking ceremonies, there is much evidence that fire walkers usually can expose themselves to great heat without pain or injury.

In the United States in the early 1980s, a man named Tolly Burkan began teaching fire walking. He claims that three hundred thousand people have walked on hot coals in fire-walking workshops since then. It is difficult to prove this one way or another.

So how do scientists try to explain fire walking? Here are some of the theories that have been put forward:
- Fire walkers have very thick or callous skin on their feet.
- The dry-wood coals used in fire walking conduct heat very poorly. The coal itself may be very hot, but it still may not transfer most of the heat to something touching it. Also, the wood coals have an uneven surface, so the actual area touching the foot is very small.
- Fire walkers keep moving rapidly. Perhaps the actual contact

time against the hot coals for each step is very small. Blood is also a good conductor of heat. The heat that does get through is quickly conducted away from the soles of the feet.

• There is something called the Leidenfrost effect. This happens when a cold, damp object, like the sole of a foot, touches a hot, dry object, like a glowing coal. The water quickly turns to steam, creating a barrier between the hot and cold objects. Since steam is a poor conductor of heat, the foot does not get burned. In "The Amateur Scientist" section of the August 1977 issue of the magazine *Scientific American,* an author describes walking across coals unharmed and attributes it to the Leidenfrost effect.

• Other explanations include self-hypnosis, applying chemicals to the skin, taking drugs to prevent pain, and many mystical or supernatural causes.

None of these explanations has been proved to the satisfaction of most scientists. The only thing that seems to be true is that some people can walk on hot coals without getting burned. How and why, we just don't know.

NOTE: FIRE WALKING IS DANGEROUS AND CAN RESULT IN SEVERE INJURIES. IT SHOULD NOT BE TRIED BY ANY READER OF THIS BOOK.

CHAPTER FOUR

# THE MYSTERIOUS TREASURE OF OAK ISLAND

**B**uried treasure is usually difficult to find. Either there are no maps that show the location or the maps are poorly drawn and inaccurate. The only mystery surrounding most hidden treasures is summed up by the word *where.*

But there is one treasure in the world that doesn't fit these rules. You can get an exact map that shows the treasure spot. You can get photographs and measurements of the burial place. And you can even get there easily by plane and boat.

The treasure is located on Oak Island, a small spot in Mahone Bay off the southern shore of Nova Scotia in Canada. The island has even become a tourist attraction, with many people visiting the site of the treasure each year.

Yet for two hundred years the buried treasure has remained on the island. Many digging expeditions have been undertaken and millions of dollars have been spent in trying to get to the treasure. But so far almost nothing has been recovered. The treasure of Oak Island remains a mystery that has not been solved.

**An aerial view of Oak Island**

The beginnings of the mystery date back to October 1795. A teenage boy, Dan McGinnis, had paddled a canoe over to Oak Island. At that time, nobody lived on the island.

McGinnis began to walk around the island through some of its oak forests. He came to a clearing and sat down to rest. Then he noticed something very odd. Beneath a large oak in the middle of the clearing, the soil had settled down into a pit several feet deep. And right above the pit, a large branch showed the remains of a pulley.

McGinnis became very excited. Could this be a spot where

treasure had been buried? The next day McGinnis returned to the island with two of his friends, Anthony Vaughan and Jack Smith. They carried picks and shovels with them.

They were convinced that treasure lay beneath the surface of the ground in the pit that McGinnis had discovered. They began to dig furiously. Hour after hour they dug down into the pit. The deeper they dug, the more excited they became. They could see that they were digging down a shaft in the hard clay soil.

It was early evening when they made the next exciting discovery. By that time they had dug down ten feet. Just below their feet they saw a platform of heavy wooden planks laid side by side. The treasure must surely be right beneath, they thought.

It was too dark to keep digging, so they decided to return the next day. Early the next morning, the boys were back at the pit. They removed the planks from the pit one by one. But instead of treasure beneath the planks, they found only more soil.

Again they began to dig, day after day. Finally they were down another ten feet, twenty feet below the surface. There they found another platform of wooden planks. But when they removed the layer of planks, they found only more soil.

They continued to dig until the winter weather prevented them from going any farther. By this time the hole was thirty feet deep. They had found still another platform of wooden planks at the thirty-foot level.

By now the boys were convinced that there must be great treasure buried in the pit. Why else would anyone dig so far down and set up the wooden platforms?

The next spring the three began to dig again. The work was much more difficult now. The pit was very deep, and all the soil had to be removed by buckets, pulleys, and ropes. Still they found no treasure, only another platform of wooden planks every ten feet down.

The digging went on for years. The boys grew up and had to take jobs to support themselves. But they dug in the pit whenever they could. Both McGinnis and Smith got married and took their brides to Oak Island to live in small houses they had built.

In 1804, nine years after the first discovery, a company was formed to dig down in the pit. The three boys, now men, worked for the company, which used all kinds of mining equipment as well as the help of other workers.

Deeper and deeper they went. Every ten feet down, they found another wooden platform laid exactly across the pit. Deeper in the shaft they found a layer of ship-waterproofing putty, then a layer of charcoal, and a third layer of a fiber that grows only in the tropics. But still they found no treasure.

The shaft was ninety-five feet deep when something new happened. The workers had finished for the day and had left. When they came back the next morning, they found that sixty feet of water had flooded the pit.

But the workers did not give up. They used buckets to try to bail out the water. Day after day they bailed. But the water level remained the same. For every bucket the workers bailed out, another bucket of water flooded in from somewhere.

Still the workers did not give up. They decided to dig another shaft nearby. Perhaps that way they could get to the level of the treasure. The new shaft went down one hundred and ten feet. But when the workers dug sideways to look for treasure, water flooded into the new shaft and filled it to the same level as in the old shaft.

That was the last straw. The company could do no more. All they had to show after months of difficult digging were two water-filled holes.

Years passed. The three original discoverers grew old. Yet they still believed in the treasure. The story of the Oak Island treasure had spread by that time. Other people began to believe that something must be buried in the "money pit."

The next big effort began in August of 1849. A group of businessmen and engineers decided to use the most modern equipment of the time to dig down in the pit.

They began to use a drill that picked up samples of whatever it passed through. At about one hundred feet, the drill went through another layer of wooden planks. Then it hit something else. It seemed to be loose metal. Was this the treasure? It is said that when the drill was brought to the surface, it contained bits of a golden chain.

But the problem of getting rid of the water remained. Finally, after months of trying to solve the water problem, the group ran out of money and quit. The treasure was still beneath the ground.

Since that time, group after group has dug in the mine. Tunnel after tunnel has been built to drain away the water. Dynamite, bulldozers, electric pumps, and all kinds of equipment have been

**The entrance to the money pit**

pressed into service. But all have failed. The water remains, and the hidden treasure has not been found.

In 1965, a tragedy struck the digging. Four people were overcome by the fumes from a motor pump and died.

Still the explorations went on. A completely new shaft was dug two hundred feet away from the money pit. This new shaft reached what seemed to be a large hole far beneath the island.

A television camera was lowered into the water-filled hole. One of the watchers claimed that he saw a chest in the dark waters. He claimed that he also saw part of a human hand.

Over the years close to fifteen different companies have tried to bring something up from the pit. At this time, the area around the pit is owned by the Triton Corporation, which maintains the dig and has opened a museum nearby. Triton is still trying to dig up whatever may be in the hole. Recent efforts have included cutting the ends off railway tanker cars and using them as liners for the pit. There have also been reports of a core drill bringing up a scrap of parchment and three links from a gold chain. The drill went to a depth of about one hundred and eighty feet.

In a new theory about Oak Island, a rival treasure hunter claims that drawing apparently random geographic features of the island on a map and then connecting them reveals a huge

**An early expedition to find out the secrets of Oak Island**

Christian cross. His theory is that a sandstone boulder and granite rocks may have been put in place as a guide to the treasure by the fourteenth-century Knights Templars.

The Templars were an order of monk-knights who fought in the Crusades and amassed great wealth. Based in southern France and loyal to the pope, the Templars became a threat to European kings. In 1307, the king of France arrested most of the Templars. The others fled and took refuge in Scotland and Portugal. There are supposedly reports that eighteen ships took the Knights Templars' treasure from France and were never seen again.

The treasure hunter claims that a member of the Knights Templars reached Nova Scotia in 1398 and built or occupied a castle at New Ross, twenty-three miles inland from Oak Island. His mission might have been to bury the Knights Templars' treasure to protect it.

To this day, no one knows for sure if there is any treasure one hundred feet or more down in the money pit. Yet someone built the shaft and put the wooden platforms in place. Why would anyone go to all that trouble unless some incredible treasure was buried there?

# GHOST SHIP

There are many stories of ghost ships at sea. Most of them are just made-up tales. Even those stories that are based on fact are usually easily explained. But there is at least one account of a ghost ship that is factual and yet very mysterious. The story concerns a sailing ship named the *Mary Celeste*.

The mystery began on the afternoon of December 4, 1872. The British sailing ship *Dei Gratia* was about six hundred miles off the coast of Portugal. The lookout reported spotting a sail on the horizon.

As the two ships drew closer, Captain David Morehouse of the *Dei Gratia* observed the other ship through his telescope and recognized it as the *Mary Celeste*. But something was clearly wrong. Some of the *Mary Celeste*'s sails were missing, and the ship was wallowing from side to side in the heavy seas. Captain Morehouse could see no one at the wheel and nobody on deck.

Morehouse hailed the ship again and again. No one answered his calls. He decided to investigate and ordered a small boat launched with a crew of three. A few minutes later the three sailors stood on the deck of the *Mary Celeste*. They stamped their feet on the deck and shouted. No answer.

The seamen went below deck and looked into the cabins, the galley, and the cargo hold. Finally they had searched the entire ship. There wasn't a person on board. The ship was drifting along without her crew.

The ship itself seemed to be in good condition. The pumps were working below deck, there were no leaks, and even the sails were in fairly good shape. The cargo, seventeen hundred casks of industrial alcohol, was still lashed in place.

A small yawl carried on the deck of the *Mary Celeste* and used as a lifeboat was gone. Also missing were some navigational instruments and some of the ship's papers. But the logbook was still in the captain's cabin. The last entry was dated November 24, almost two weeks earlier. It gave no hint of any trouble.

The crew must have abandoned the *Mary Celeste* in a great hurry. The captain had left the logbook and his clothing. The crew had left not only their clothing and other personal belongings but had even left behind their pipes and tobacco. It was common knowledge that sailors would leave their tobacco behind only if they were in great danger.

But what could that danger have been? The boarders could find absolutely nothing wrong with the ship. There was plenty of

**The ghost ship** *Mary Celeste*

food and drinking water on board. It's true that sailors abandon burning or sinking ships at sea. But why abandon an undamaged ship?

Even if the *Mary Celeste* had been caught in a storm, the large ship would still have been safer than the smaller lifeboat. And there was no sign of a fire on board or any other damage. In fact, the boarding party of three seamen was able to sail the *Mary Celeste* six hundred miles to Gibraltar all by themselves.

Could pirates have boarded the ship and done away with the crew? Could there have been a mutiny? Neither seemed likely. In either case there should have been signs of a struggle. But there were none. Pirates would have taken more than just a few instruments. Mutineers would certainly have taken their clothing and tobacco along with them. There just seemed to be no reason for the crew to be gone.

Even before the *Mary Celeste* was found abandoned, the ship seemed to be unlucky. She had been built in Nova Scotia and launched in 1861. Her original name was the *Amazon*. Her first captain died two days after he took command. On her first voyage, she suffered damage to her hull. While the damage was being repaired, fire broke out aboard ship. Her second captain lost his job because of these misfortunes.

Her third captain sailed her across the Atlantic—and promptly ran into another ship in the Strait of Dover. She was repaired once again and sailed home with still another captain. A few years later, the *Amazon* ran aground on Cape Breton Island and was badly damaged.

This time the *Amazon* was completely rebuilt and sold to new owners. They renamed her the *Mary Celeste* and planned to sail her under an American flag. Her new captain was Benjamin Spooner Briggs. He was just thirty-eight years old but had spent most of those years at sea. He had been captain of three previous ships and had the reputation of being a good sailor.

Briggs and Captain Morehouse of the *Dei Gratia* were good friends. They dined together the night before the *Mary Celeste* was to sail. Briggs took his wife and infant daughter along with him on the newly rebuilt ship's first voyage. He certainly did not seem nervous or describe anything wrong.

Weeks later, when Captain Morehouse found the abandoned *Mary Celeste,* he may have felt sorry for his friend Captain Briggs. But Morehouse knew that the *Mary Celeste* would bring him a good profit. Under the laws of the sea, Morehouse could claim a part of the value of the abandoned ship and its cargo.

Morehouse's friendship with Briggs seemed suspicious to the attorney general of Gibraltar. He decided to try to prove that Morehouse was responsible for whatever had happened to the *Mary Celeste.* But there was very little evidence of that. In fact, the attorney general could come up with only three bits of possible foul play. First, there was a small cut in the ship's railing. Second, Briggs's sword, found beneath his bunk, had a few rust spots that might have been blood. And third, the last log entry had been made hundreds of miles from where the *Mary Celeste* had been found.

The members of the naval court of inquiry were not impressed by the supposed evidence. The cut railing could have been an accident. The spots on the sword did not even look like blood. And ships' logs were often made out days later than they should have been. Besides, there was no sign of any struggle at all. Captain Morehouse and his crew were quickly cleared of any wrongdoing.

The naval court was also supposed to come up with an opinion on what really happened to the *Mary Celeste.* But after three months of investigations they could find no evidence of any kind. They admitted that they could find no explanation for the disappearance of Captain Briggs and his crew.

In the years that followed, all kinds of explanations were offered as to what happened to the *Mary Celeste*. Some said that the ship was attacked by monsters from the depths of the sea, such as giant squids or whales or even more fearsome creatures. Others thought that sickness aboard ship or pirates of one kind or another were responsible. More recent explanations involve the crew being abducted by UFOs or visitors from outer space.

About the time of the trial, the *Mary Celeste*'s owner came up with an explanation that at least seems possible. He suggested that some of the alcohol in the cargo may have leaked. Hot weather might have evaporated the alcohol and built up enough gas pressure to blow open the hatch cover.

Captain Briggs may have mistakenly thought that a fire caused the explosion. He might have ordered the crew to abandon ship at once. The small lifeboat could have been swamped in the rough seas. This would leave the ship empty and yet perfectly sound.

But any explosion could not have been a large one, because there was no evidence of damage. In fact, there is nothing to prove that any part of this explanation is correct. No one has ever been able to come up with a satisfactory explanation. To this day, the disappearance of the crew of the *Mary Celeste* remains one of the most puzzling sea mysteries of all time.

# CHAPTER SIX

# THE CRYSTAL SKULL

For many years, the Museum of the American Indian in New York City had an unusual object on display. It was a life-size sculpture of a human skull carved from a single piece of quartz, or rock crystal. As the crystal skull turned slowly on its rotating base, it glittered and sparkled like a huge diamond.

But the crystal skull was more than just a beautiful object of art. Some people thought that the skull was surrounded by a strange halo of its own light at certain times. They thought that the skull gave off silvery, bell-like sounds; that strange images would appear inside the skull; and that a peculiar smell was sometimes given off. These people even insisted that the skull had the power to influence a person's mood and thoughts.

The discovery of the skull itself is shrouded in mystery. It was reported to have been found in 1927 in an ancient city called Lubaantum, built by the Maya. The skull was found beneath a collapsed altar by Anna Mitchell-Hedges. She was the adopted

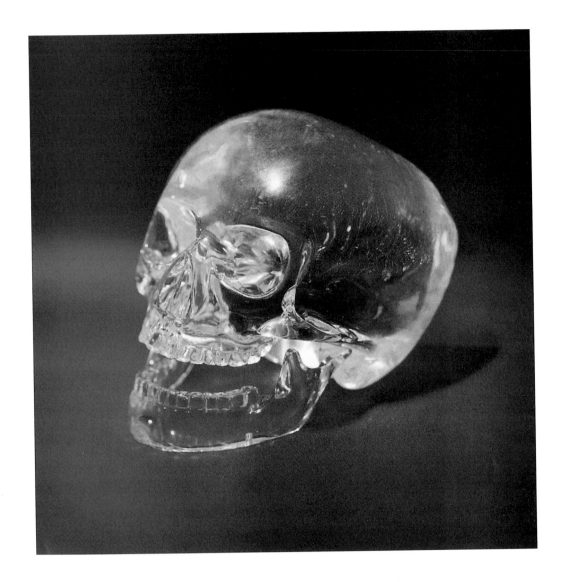

daughter of the British explorer Frederick A. Mitchell-Hedges.

Mitchell-Hedges had spent years searching Central America for Lubaantum and also for evidence of the mythical lost civilization of Atlantis. He had finally found the ruined city of Lubaantum in the jungles of Belize, then called British Honduras.

Mitchell-Hedges writes in his autobiography that Anna discovered the skull on her seventeenth birthday.

The crystal skull looks different from other pieces of art found in Mayan cities. While many carved Mayan skulls have been found, none is made with quite the same skill. Most other Mayan skulls are made from clay, wood, bone, or shell. But the Mitchell-Hedges skull is the only life-size crystal skull with movable parts, and its workmanship is far better than that of other crystal skulls.

The skull is beautifully made from clear rock crystal. Within the crystal are veins and bubbles that were formed millions of years ago, when the piece of quartz first became a hardened mineral. The skull seems to have been carved without the use of metal tools, since no scratches or tool marks have been seen under microscopic examination.

The surface of the crystal skull is as smooth as glass. That itself is a mystery. Rock crystal is a very hard mineral. If the surface had been smoothed by being rubbed down with sand, it would have taken hundreds of years of constant work by generations of artisans.

The lower jaw of the skull is a separate piece of quartz. The jaw fits tightly into two polished sockets and can be moved up and down so that it looks like the mouth is opening and closing. Channels have been hollowed out in the skull, reaching from the bottom to the eye sockets. If a light is placed beneath the skull, it makes the eyes flicker in an eerie way.

The skull measures about five inches high by seven inches long and five inches wide. It weighs eleven pounds, seven ounces. If it were to be sold, it would fetch at least several hundred thousand dollars. But for many people it is truly priceless.

Ever since the skull was first discovered, its discoverer and other people who have examined it have claimed that it has some strange powers. Anna Mitchell-Hedges said that when she found the skull, three hundred Indians who were working with her father fell to their knees and kissed the ground. Then they prayed and wept around the spot for two weeks.

In 1956, Frank Dorland, an art expert, started to study the skull and conduct tests on it. For six years he studied the skull and tried to find out what it was and what its properties were. Some of his claims about the skull are very surprising and even frightening.

For example, Dorland claimed that when he kept the skull in his house for study, weird things began to happen. When he went to sleep, he and wife were awakened by unusual noises in the house. They heard what sounded like a large jungle cat prowling through the house. They also heard the sounds of chimes and bells.

Dorland went on to state that when he awoke the next morning, the rooms in his house were in a mess, with his things strewn about all over. But the windows to the rooms were all closed and locked.

Anna Mitchell-Hedges said that her father thought that the skull was an evil thing. He believed that the skull brought death to those people who laughed at its powers. One legend about the skull says that the Mayan high priest used the skull as an instrument to will an enemy to death.

In the March 1962 issue of *Fate Magazine* there is an article that says that the temperature of the skull always remains the same. It seems to keep a steady temperature of about seventy degrees Fahrenheit. Even when the skull is placed in a refrigerator, it comes out still showing a reading of seventy degrees. This extraordinary claim has not been proved by any independent scientific investigation.

Dorland and other persons who viewed the skull when he was studying it insisted that the skull changed its appearance from time to time. Its color changed from clear crystal to shades of green, violet, purple, red, blue, and amber. It also sometimes had a heavy odor like that of moist earth.

According to Dorland, people observing the skull heard all kinds of noises, from chimes and bells to what sounded like soft human voices. Observers also experienced tightness in their muscles and a rise in pulse rate and blood pressure.

It is difficult to know what to make of all these claims of supernatural powers. Most of them cannot be proved or disproved. One thing that can be said is that when the skull was displayed at the Museum of the American Indian, no special powers were noticed by any observers. Perhaps the skull is such a beautiful and unusual object that all the strange happenings really occurred only in the minds of the observers.

As for the questions about who made the skull or when it was made, no proof has been advanced one way or another. Most observers are fairly sure that the skull is Mayan or Aztec, and they assume the honesty of the story of the find by the Mitchell-Hedges family.

Mayan and Aztec skulls of wood, bone, shell, and ceramic have often been found. But the Mitchell-Hedges skull is unique in many ways that have nothing to do with any supposed supernatural properties it may possess. Its detail and craftsmanship are far superior to that of any other Indian skull. No other life-size crystal skull with a movable jaw has ever been found.

The skull was examined closely by the Hewlett-Packard crystal laboratories in Santa Clara, California. (Hewlett-Packard manufactured tiny quartz crystals for use in watches and other instruments.) The laboratory determined that the skull and the lower jaw were each carved from single pieces of rock crystal (quartz). Rock crystal is so hard that it is difficult to carve. Hewlett–Packard estimated that it would have taken three hundred years of effort to produce a skull of that size and grind it smooth.

The skull also has many interesting light properties. If a laser beam is directed at a point in the middle of the nose cavity, the entire skull becomes fully lighted. By shifting a light or by walking around the skull, many different patterns of light changes can be seen. Some of the laboratory people felt that the lenses and prisms in the skull show a knowledge of optics that has only recently been understood.

Perhaps in the future the crystal skull will be studied further by scientists and more will be found out. Until that time, the crystal skull remains a beautiful and mysterious relic of an age long past.

# CHAPTER SEVEN

# STRANGE BOOMS

It was an ordinary December weekday in Charleston, South Carolina. By midmorning, children were in school, stores were full of shoppers, and the streets were crowded with traffic.

Suddenly, the peaceful day was shattered by a boom that shook windows and startled the people. What was the cause of the strange boom? Nobody seemed to know. There were no explosions that anyone knew about, no smoke to be seen, and no other effects after the boom.

The people in Charleston slowly returned to their business. Whatever had caused the boom seemed to be gone now.

But that afternoon, people in parts of New Jersey, New York, and Connecticut felt and heard still another strange boom. And this boom was even recorded on scientific air-pressure measuring instruments at the Lamont-Doherty Observatory in Palisades, New Jersey.

Later, Dr. William Donn, chief of the observatory's atmospheric sciences department, commented on the boom. He said that it was the strongest atmospheric sound ever recorded at his laboratory. The sound drove the needle right off the upper end of the scale.

Dr. Donn said that the source of the boom seemed to be directly south of the Palisades observatory, but that the instruments could not measure how far away it was. He said that the source of the boom was probably something in the atmosphere rather than on or beneath the ocean's surface.

All kinds of possible causes were presented by different people. Perhaps the blasts were sonic booms caused by airplanes such as the Concorde SST or military jets. Perhaps they were test explosions at offshore oil rigs or the sound of earthquakes at sea. Still other explanations ranged from Soviet submarine missile tests to satellite reentries into the atmosphere to meteors. Of course, some people immediately said that the booms were caused by UFOs.

But whatever caused the booms that December day in 1977 had not just disappeared. More booms continued to be heard during the following year. And when scientists began to look for the causes, they found that strange booms are a centuries-old mystery.

Many of the reports date from much quieter times, when there were no jet aircraft (or indeed any aircraft at all) and very little blasting of any kind. Here are just a few of the many reports on unexplained booms.

In 1846, the magazine *Scientific American* printed an article about strange sounds heard in the town of Deerfield, New Hampshire. For twelve years there had been reports of strange explosions in the ground that frightened the townspeople. The sounds were heard at all hours of the night and during the day, and in winter as well as in summer.

Recently, the article went on to say, the sounds had grown louder and louder. As many as twenty booms had been heard in one night. "Many of them jar the houses and ground, so much so, that a child whose balance is not steady will roll from one side to the other. They are as loud as a heavy cannon fired near a house." The sounds even caused a stone wall to fall over and also caused the cave-in of a stone cellar.

In 1895 and 1896, the French scientific magazine *Ciel et terre* (Sky and Earth) listed several hundred pages of reports on what they called *mistpouffers,* or "fog guns." *Mistpouffers* was one of the names given to dull, distant booms heard around the coast of Europe all the way to Iceland. Each country had a different name for the sounds, and there were many reports from Europe and also from places along the coasts of North America and Asia.

India in the 1890s was the scene of some of the most famous booming sounds. These sounds were heard by millions of people along the Ganges River. The repeated blasts sounded like distant thunder or the rumble of artillery and were known as the Barisal Guns. They were named after the headquarters of a district in which the sounds were heard most clearly and most often.

The Barisal Guns were heard mostly from February to October during rainy weather. The sounds always came in threes, one after another. Similar stories came from Seneca Lake in New York and New Brunswick in Canada.

Another report of Barisal Guns, this time from Australia, was printed in the magazine *Nature* in 1908. Here is part of that story: "A peculiar incident happened here last evening about an hour after sunset. In a south-easterly direction from here three reports took place high up in the air, and then a rushing noise like steam escaping, lasting for a few seconds, and gradually dying away.... It was a beautiful clear evening, and there was nothing visible at all in that direction."

There are reports of unexplained booming sounds in country after country throughout the world. Yet all of these reports seemed of little interest to scientists until the booms heard along the Atlantic coast in 1977.

The United States Naval Research Laboratory in Washington, D.C., then established a team of scientists that collected reports about the mystery booms. They looked over instrument readings from the Lamont-Doherty Observatory as well as reports from people on the street who had heard the sounds.

Almost immediately, the naval scientists ruled out several explanations. Chemical or nuclear tests and high explosives were very unlikely to have been the cause of the sounds, the scientists said. That is because there was no evidence of any tests that took place during the time the booms were heard.

The Concorde SST was not a likely cause of the sounds. Many of the booms were heard when the nearest Concordes were on the ground and the others far too distant. In addition, the booms were too loud and did not sound like sonic booms caused by jets.

Then just what did cause the booms? The scientists were unsure. They thought that different booms might have had different causes. Some of the theories they explored were that the booms might have been caused by explosions of methane gas at the bottom of the sea or by movements within the earth's crust.

Whatever the reason for the booms, at least this much is certain: The strange sounds were real, not imaginary. Perhaps one day *mistpouffers* and Barisal Guns will no longer be a mystery.

# CHAPTER EIGHT

# PHOTOGRAPHING THE INVISIBLE

There is an invisible halo that surrounds living things and even some nonliving and dead things. But while everybody agrees that this unseen halo can be photographed, scientists and other people disagree about just what causes the ghost images in the photos.

One investigator, Alfred Hulstrunk, a biologist, claimed to be able to photograph the emotions of a person. Using a special technique, he made color movies of a subject's halo. The movies, he said, show a change in color when the subject feels love or anger. He went on to say that love shows up as a pink and blue halo around a person, while anger shows up mostly as red.

Another investigator was Thelma Moss, a clinical psychologist. She took photographs of seeds, leaves, people, and rats. She believed that she could take a photograph of a seed and tell not only whether the seed would sprout but where the roots would grow. She said that she was dealing with a "life force."

Research with this kind of photography began in 1939 in

Russia. A Soviet scientist named Semyon Kirlian found that he could use high voltages to make a photograph with just film—no camera. Kirlian and his wife spent the next forty years working on high-voltage, or "Kirlian," photography, as it began to be called.

To make a Kirlian photograph, an object is placed between two metal plates. Photographic film in a lightproof envelope is placed beneath one of the plates. A high-voltage alternating current is applied to the plates. This results in a Kirlian image appearing on the film when it is developed.

In the case of some objects—including an animal or a part of a human, such as a finger—only one plate and the film are used. The animal itself is grounded, and this completes the system.

Kirlian photographs can be taken in color or in black and white. They usually show a bright halo around a person. The Kirlians and some other investigators believe that the variations in the size, shape, and color of the halo depend upon how the person is feeling that particular day.

Some of the results reported by members of the International Kirlian Research Association (IKRA) certainly sound very startling. For example, Thelma Moss and K. L. Johnson took Kirlian photographs of the fingertips of some five hundred people. They found that the photos showed a particular kind of halo around each person's fingertip. And these halos varied at different times according to the person's emotional state.

Another report from IKRA states that changes in the Kirlian halo can occur as a result of cancer and other diseases, even before these illnesses can be detected in other ways. For example, a cancerous area may show a different color or size in the halo around that spot. However, other scientists say that different studies show no relation between Kirlian photographs and any diseases.

Some Soviet investigators discovered what they called the

phantom effect. They took Kirlian photographs of a leaf after a part of it had been cut away. They said that the photographs still show the outline of the original leaf. The cut-away part is fainter than the rest but still visible. Some Russian writers claim that this phantom leaf proves that there is a special life force in living things.

Most scientists think that these reports of phantoms or life forces are just nonsense. They say that the photographs of strange lights around an object are due to electrical causes of various kinds and not the emotional state of the subject.

For example, a study by scientists at Drexel University and Villanova University was published in the magazine *Science*. The scientists wrote that the variations in Kirlian photographs are the result of differing amounts of moisture the subjects transfer to the photographic film when they touch it. The moisture causes changes in the electric-charge pattern of the film. As a result, the Kirlian photographs show changes in the image of the subject.

Kirlian photography is useful, these scientists said. If properly controlled, it is a good way of finding and measuring the moisture content of objects. In other words, it can be used to find slight amounts of water.

Scientists at the Lawrence Livermore Laboratory in California found another use for Kirlian photography: testing materials for hidden defects. The high-voltage photographs they made showed defects that were invisible in ordinary photos.

Most scientists and scientific agencies are simply not interested in Kirlian photography. They believe that there is very little about

it that is worth the money to investigate. The National Science Foundation and the National Institutes of Health have not invested any time or money in the field.

Scientists find little truth in the idea that any sort of aura or life force exists around people or plants, as supposedly shown in Kirlian photographs. The most damaging evidence against the life-force claim is that Kirlian photography works on *any* subject that conducts electricity, even completely lifeless metal or synthetic sponges soaked in salt water, which makes the sponges conduct electricity.

The Kirlian field jumps around as you look at it. You can actually see it in a darkened room. Because the shape of the field changes, it sometimes appears to outline nonexistent parts of the subject, thus giving the phantom effect. In fact, researchers often get false phantom effects, the appearance of pieces of a subject that have never existed. Some investigators would still like to use the technique of high-voltage photography in industry. Whatever it is called, Kirlian photography is still of interest to some people.

# CHAPTER NINE

# LIGHTS IN THE NIGHT

People often report seeing mysterious lights in the night sky. Until they are identified, these lights can be referred to as Unidentified Flying Objects (UFOs for short). If you are out one night and see a light moving in the sky and cannot identify it as a star, planet, airplane, or other object, then it is by definition a UFO. Does this mean that you have seen an alien spacecraft? Probably not. The vast majority of UFO reports can be explained without difficulty as natural or human-made objects misidentified for one reason or another.

Some sky lights are auroras borealis, sometimes called northern lights. Auroras are caused by the earth's magnetic field and a sudden increase in radiation from the sun. Other lights in the night sky may be caused by lightning flashes or clouds reflecting searchlights or lights from a nearby city.

Sometimes the entire night sky brightens. The glows probably result from dust given off by a large volcanic eruption or a big explosion of some kind. For example, sky glows were reported for

**Lights in the sky**

days after the Tunguska explosion in Siberia (see chapter 2).

The actual percentage of so-called UFOs that can be explained is ninety to ninety-five percent. But some reports of strange lights in the night do not seem to fit within any of the usual groups. Some of these lights are seen in the same place on different nights, sometimes for years. The lights may change in size and color. At times a few lights are seen, at other times many lights. Sometimes they even seem to disappear when chased. What about these few remaining cases? The best that scientists can say is that they don't know what they are, but that there is absolutely no proof that they are alien spacecraft.

One famous light, called the Palatine Light, has been reported by many reliable observers through the years. The name comes from a ship that burned and sank just off Block Island. In common with many of the reports of strange lights, the Palatine Light sounds much like a ghost story.

According to *A History of Block Island,* by Samuel Livermore, the light is seen offshore but is bright enough to light up the walls of a room through a window. Block Island natives are so familiar with the light that they do not give it a second thought, unless some off-islander asks about it.

Observers describe the Palatine Light as changing in size and brightness. Sometimes it is small, while at other times it becomes as large as a full-masted sailing ship. When it is at its largest, the light looks as if something is on fire, giving off shining rays in all directions.

Another "ghostly" light was reported in a Charlotte, North Carolina, newspaper in the mid-1970s. The light was first seen by some young people on an old road near swampy land. The light changed color and shape and seemed to move up and down the road. It was chased by automobiles at speeds up to sixty miles per hour but was never caught. One observer said he saw the light sitting on the hood of his car. Another heard the faint tinkling of a bell. When the light appeared, the bell began ringing like mad.

Some scientists think that they have a good explanation for some of these strange lights, particularly those that are seen near swamps. In swamps or marshy places, gases such as methane are released by rotting plant materials. These marsh gases sometimes light up, either by electrical discharges during thunderstorms or just by spontaneous combustion. When that happens, shiny globes of fire may appear in the swamp.

Sometimes the lights look like tiny flames right on the ground, and other times the flames rise and float in the air. The flames go out in one place and suddenly appear in another, making it look as if they are in motion. The lights may be yellow, red, or blue-green. The lights do not burn or char the ground, and they seem to give off little heat.

The marsh lights are seen so often that they have even been given common names in different places. They are called jack-o'-lanterns, will-o'-the-wisps, or foolish fire. The lights can appear for hours at a stretch, and sometimes for a whole night. Usually there is no smell. Sometimes there is a popping sound, like the little explosion when a gas burner ignites. It seems clear that at least some of the reports of "ghostly" lights are probably sightings of marsh gas.

Still other sky glows—floods of light, sheets of lightning, and other strange lights—are often reported as being seen before, during, and after earthquakes. For many years most scientists paid little attention to these reports. But recently the reports have been studied in some detail by scientists of the United States Geological Survey.

For example, thousands of eyewitness reports of earthquake lights were collected in the 1930s in Japan. The lights were described as looking like sheet lightning, meteors, electric sparks, fireballs, streamers, and beams or columns of light. Some people said that the clouds were lit up by a strange red glow. The lights were seen for more than fifty miles before, during, and even for some time after the quakes.

A Japanese physics professor collected photographs of lights seen during earthquakes from 1965 to 1967. The photographs clearly show that earthquake lights are real and not just an illusion. In the terrible 1976 earthquake in Tangshan, China, the lights brightened the night sky so that it looked like daylight.

No one is exactly sure what causes earthquake lights. Perhaps there are several different causes. Lights described as looking like electric sparks or meteors may be caused by earthquake effects on power lines or electric generating plants. Another theory is that certain kinds of rocks in the earth produce electrical charges when they are violently moved during a quake. The charges might result in lightninglike flashes that light up the sky.

Of course, not all sightings of strange lights in the night can be explained, and these reports continue to come in from all over the world. The Palatine Light, for example, has yet to be explained. Mysterious lights seen by many people in the skies of northern Michigan in 1992 and 1993 also remain unexplained. Different observers of the Michigan lights reported "loud noises…orange colors in the sky," "Frisbee-shaped objects with zigzagging colorful lights," and "a series of lights,…maybe four or five,…[and] an orange color."

In June 1995, a newspaper in Fairfield, California, noted many local sightings of "orange streaking lights and strange circular objects" that seemed to be hovering over the town. According to amateur UFO watchers, the area around Fairfield is the center of a grid of magnetic lines that, they say, is "hot" for UFO sightings.

Project Blue Book was organized in 1952 by the air force to investigate strange lights in the sky. The project's panel was made up of physicists, engineers, meteorologists, and an astronomer. They had three main goals: to explain all of the sightings of UFOs, to decide if UFOs posed a threat to the country, and to determine whether UFOs were using advanced technology. The scientists examined thousands of records of sightings, including photo documentation and interviews with people who claimed to have seen a UFO.

Most of the sightings turned out to be well-known objects, such as stars or bright planets like Venus or Jupiter, or such events as auroras or meteors making trails as they fell through the atmosphere. Many other sightings turned out to be weather balloons, satellites, aircraft lights, or large flights of migratory birds.

In February 1966, another panel of scientists issued a report that stated that almost all UFO sightings could be explained as either natural events or outright hoaxes. A few scientists disagreed with the panel's conclusions. This group included James E. McDonald, a meteorologist at the University of Arizona, and J. Allen Hynek, an astronomer at Northwestern University.

McDonald and Hynek maintained that because a few reliable UFO reports had never been clearly explained, it was almost certain that earth was being visited by extraterrestrials.

Most scientists disagreed with McDonald and Hynek. In 1968, Edward Condon, a physicist at the University of Colorado, headed a panel of thirty-seven scientists who studied fifty-nine UFO sightings and all the supporting physical and photographic evidence. The committee's final report, "A Scientific Study of UFOs," was released in 1969. The Condon Report concluded that there was absolutely no evidence of extraterrestrial control of UFOs and also that no further UFO studies were needed.

Project Blue Book was closed in December 1969. By the time the project ended, it had recorded eighty thousand pages of information on 12,618 reported UFO sightings and events. Each of these was classified as either "identified," with a known astronomical or atmospheric cause, or "unidentified," without enough information to determine the cause. Five to ten percent of the sightings were, in the end, classified as unidentified.

Some astronomers are convinced that there may be forms of life on other planets in our galaxy. They think that there *might* be intelligent life out there somewhere. SETI (Search for Extraterrestrial Intelligence) programs are "listening" to stars in the hope of detecting radio signals that might indicate intelligent life. But so far nothing has been found.

Even if there is intelligent life on other planets, it is not likely that life-forms from these planets could reach earth. At the speed

**This photograph of strange lights in the sky was taken during an earthquake that occurred in Japan.**

of our fastest spaceships, it would take seventy thousand *years* to journey to earth from the nearest star—and the return trip would take just as long! Of course, modern technology may soon allow for faster space travel, but it does seem unlikely that we are being visited and not even informed about it by our visitors.

There are so many thousands of UFO reports that it is difficult for scientists to explain every one of them. But a UFO is just that: an *Unidentified* Flying Object. Just because an object is unidentified does not mean that it is automatically a spaceship from Mars.

It is difficult if not impossible to prove that alien spaceships do *not* exist. But proving that *anything* does not exist is difficult. For example, how do you go about proving that blue polka-dotted giraffes do not exist? Just because nobody has ever seen such a giraffe does not really prove that none exist.

Scientists say that the case for alien visitors from other planets is not up to the scientists to disprove but up to its supporters to prove. And most scientists feel that the case has simply not been proved. There is just not enough clear and convincing evidence that scientists can look at and examine.

When a blue polka-dotted giraffe shows up in a zoo, scientists will believe that such an animal exists. And when an alien spaceship lands on the White House lawn, scientists will be happy to greet the visitors.